THE 'OFFICIAL'

CB

SLANGUAGE

LANGUAGE

DICTIONARY

INCLUDING

CROSS-REFERENCE

by
Lanie Dills

D1264404

Lanie Dills, Nashville, Tennessee, Publisher

Robert M. Silver,
LOUIS J. MARTIN & ASSOCIATES, INC.
95 Madison Avenue, New York, N.Y. 10016
Distributors to the trade.

First Edition
©Lanie Dills, 1975

Revised Edition
© Lanie Dills, 1976

First printing - December, 1975
Second printing - January, 1976
Third printing, revised edition - March, 1976
Fourth printing-March, 1976

Library of Congress Catalog Card Number:
  LC 76-4130
ISBN 0-916744-00-0
Printed in the United States of America

DEDICATION

To: Tim
          Cita
Real Friends
Close Family

TABLE OF CONTENTS

INTRODUCTION

Recognizing that CB jargon is like a foreign language to the beginning CBer, we intend this dictionary and cross-reference to provide a quick and easy guide for learning CB slanguage.

Since CB slanguage does vary greatly from section to section of the country, and because it continues to expand rapidly, keeping pace with today's CB boom, we hope that the reference will be a "must" to the long time CBer who wishes to be knowledgeable in current CB terminology used throughout the nation.

Additionally, THE 'OFFICIAL' CB SLANGUAGE LANGUAGE DICTIONARY AND CROSS-REFERENCE will prove invaluable to those who do not actively talk on the CB, but who nevertheless are interested in acquiring an understanding of CB's fascinatingly colorful lingo.

The pages of this reference contain terminology from every section of the country. Thousands of travelled miles and literally thousands of monitored conversations, both base and mobile, have produced the bulk of the material. Much of the balance was obtained from interviews with individual CBers and groups of CBers across the country.

Compiling the book was at once interesting hard

work and continuously exciting fun. It is hoped that the reader will find the dictionary and cross-reference a novel amusement and also a useful tool for learning and interpreting CB slanguage.

The slanguage of CB is steadily growing and new terms are born daily. If you have a new term which you would like to see included in a subsequent revision of this work, please fill in and return the form located on page 127.—Lanie Dills

BEGINNER'S GUIDE TO TRANSMISSION

Initially, most beginners are afraid to talk on the CB because they are unfamiliar with CB slanguage. Beginners are usually somewhat embarrassed by their first efforts and they suffer from a condition commonly known as "mike fright". The information provided below should serve as a helpful guide for new CBers in the first difficult stages.

I. INITIAL TRANSMISSIONS

The first item to remember when making a transmission is that you must, according to FCC Rules, identify yourself by your callsign, a combination of letters and numbers given to you upon your request for a license. In addition, you may wish to use frequent CB terms, such as "break", "breaker broke", or "break 10 (channel number)". Also, you may choose to identify yourself by your *handle*, your CB code name.

Sample: "Break 10. This is KXL-5375, the Nashville Popsicle."

You may have a number of purposes for breaking into the channel. Below we have listed some of the most frequent ones and the common terms to signify them.

A. <u>To call a specific person:</u>
    COLLECT CALL

    BREAK FOR *(individual's callsign and handle)*

LONG DISTANCE TELEPHONE IS RINGING FOR *(individual's callsign and handle)*

Sample: "This is KXL-5375, the Nashville Popsicle; I have a collect call for that Sugar Britches."

B. <u>To transmit emergency information</u>   (transmission should be made on Channel 9, the channel officially disignated and monitored for emergency traffic):

MAYDAY

10-34 (official ten-code number to indicate emergency)

10-33 (abbreviated ten-code number)

Sample: "Break Channel nine. We've got a 10-33 on I40 at Exit 215."

C. <u>To obtain police location and road condition reports:</u>

BEAR STORY

FIX

LEFT SHOULDER

SMOKEY REPORT

Sample: "Breaker, KXI-7248, Sugar Britches here, looking for a westbound 18 wheeler. How does it look over your left shoulder?"

D. To obtain directions:

Give your location (what the CBers call your *twenty*) and the location desired.

Sample: "Break 10. This is KXI-7248, The Sugar Britches. I'm at Interstate 40, exit 215. How do I get to White's Creek Road?"

E. To obtain a radio check:

METER READING

COPY

POUNDS ("S" units on meter)

10-32

Sample: "Break 10 for a radio check. This is KXI-7248. How many pounds am I putting on you?"

F. To obtain correct time:

10-34 (abbreviated ten-code)

10-36 (official ten-code)

Sample: "KXI-7248, Sugar Britches here, breaking for a 10-36."

II. SEEKING RESPONSES

Several terms indicate that you wish someone to respond to you. Perhaps the most common are:

COME BACK

COME ON

GO AHEAD

GO BREAKER

WE'RE LISTENING

Sample: "KXL-5375, the Nashville Popsicle here. Come back on that radio check."

III. SIGNOFF

As in the initial transmission, you should sign off with your call sign. But in addition, you may wish to indicate that you will be listening or leaving the air entirely.

A.   Through talking but monitoring:

EARS ON

COPYING THE MAIL

DOWN AND ON THE SIDE

LAY OVER AND LISTEN

ON STANDBY

10-10

Sample: "The one Nashville Popsicle, KXI-5375. We're down and on the side."

B. <u>Through talking and leaving the air:</u>

ADIOS

CLEAR

CUT LOOSE

GONE

OUT

Sample: "KXL-5375, we're clear."

DICTIONARY

KEY: MW - mid-western U.S.
       NE - northeast U.S.
       NW - northwest U.S.
       SE - southeast U.S.
       SW - southwest U.S.
        W - western U.S.

ADIOS: sign-off; finished talking (SW).

ADVERTISING: a marked police car that has its lights turned on.

AF: audio frequency.

AFFIRMATIVE: yes.

ALERT: Affiliated League of Emergency Radio Teams.

AMPLITUDE MODULATION (AM): a technique of varying the power output so it can be used for conveying messages.

ANL: automatic noise limiter; a device in most CB rigs to reduce ignition noise interference.

APPLES: CBers who operate illegally.

ASTRODOME CITY: Houston, Texas (SE).

B.R. TOWN: Baton Rouge, La.

BACK: over; back to you.

BACK 'EM UP: slow down; stop transmitting(SE).

BACK 'EM ON DOWN or UP: stop transmitting; slow down (SE).

BACK IT ON OUT: stop transmitting.

BACK OFF: stop transmitting; slow down.

BACK OFF ON IT: slow down (SE).

BACK OFF THE HAMMER: slow down (SE).

BACK ON DOWN: stop transmitting; slow down (SE).

BACK OUT: stop transmitting.

BACK OUT OF IT: stop transmitting; slow down.

BACK TO YOU: answer back; e.g. "You've got the Sugar Britches back to you."

BACKDOOR: last CB vehicle in a group of two or more.

BACKDOOR CLOSED: rear covered for police.

BACKDOOR SEALED UP: rear CBer will notify if police are on the move from behind.

BACKGROUND: noise preventing clear transmission.

BACKSLIDE: return trip (SE); e.g. "Definitely did enjoy the rachet jawing; we'll catch you on the backslide."

BACKSTROKE: return trip (SE).

BACKYARD: the road behind; e.g. "Take a look in your backyard, good buddy, and give me a bear report."

BAGGING THEM: police catching speeders (NE).

BANG A UEY: make a U turn (NE).

BAR CITY: Forrest City, Arkansas (SE).

BAREFOOT: legal operation of CB in terms of power; e.g. "Hey, good buddy, are you sure you're running barefoot in that mobile? You're blowing my windows out."

BAREFOOT MOBILE: mobile CB rig with no extra power.

BARLEY POP: beer (NW).

BARN: truck garage.

BARNIES: police (SW).

BARYPHONY: speech difficulty.

BASEMENT: Channel 1 (NW); e.g. "Too many rachet jawers on this channel, let's go to the basement."

BASE STATION: transceiver installed at a fixed location and primarily used for communicating with mobile units and other base stations.

BASKETBALL ON CHANNEL 9: monitoring Channel 9 (SE).

BAY CITY: San Francisco, California (W).

BEAM: a type of antenna which is highly directional.

BEAN TOWN: Boston, Massachusetts (NE).

BEAR BAIT: speeding car without CB (SE); e.g. "Here comes some bear bait 'round ya, let them feed the bears at Exit 84."

BEAR BAIT PASSENGER: car without CB which will speed past and be caught by police (SE).

BEAR BITE: speeding ticket (SE).

BEAR BUSTER: a CB converter which is installed on an AM car radio and permits monitoring of CB conversation.

BEAR CAGE: police station.

BEAR CAVE: police or highway patrol station (W).

BEAR FOOD: speeding vehicle without CB.

BEAR IN THE AIR: police helicopter.

BEAR IN THE SKY: police helicopter.

BEAR MEAT: speeding car without CB.

BEAR REPORT: police location report, e.g. "How about an Eastbound 18 wheeler, we need a bear report, good buddy."

BEAR STORY: police location report (SE); e.g. "How about that Eastbound side? Tell me a bear story."

BEAR TRAP: radar set-up.

BEARDED BUDDY: police of any kind (SE).

BEARS: police of any kind.

BEARS ARE CRAWLING: police or troopers are switching from side to side of the expressway (SE).

BEAR'S DEN: police station.

BEAT THE BUSHES: "front door" (lead vehicle) looks for Smokey and warns CBers behind him of Smokey's position.

BEAVER: woman or girl (SE).

BEER CITY: Milwaukee, Wisconsin (MW).

BENDING THE WINDOWS: clear reception of signal (SE).

BETTER COOL IT: slow down.

BIG A: Amarillo, Texas (SW); Atlanta, Georgia (SE).

BIG BROTHER: police of any kind.

BIG CAR: tractor trailer truck.

BIG EARS: clear reception of signal.

BIG D: Dallas, Texas (SW).

BIG DOG: Greyhound bus.

BIG M: Memphis, Tennessee (SE).

BIG R: trucks belonging to Roadway Freight System (SE); e.g. "How about ya, Big R. Got your ears on?"

BIG SLAB: expressway (SE).

BIG SWITCH: turning off the CB set.

BIG T: Tucson, Arizona (SW).

BIKINI STATE: Florida.

BIRD: Ford Thunderbird.

BIRD IN THE AIR: police helicopter (SE).

BIT ON THE SEAT OF THE BRITCHES: got a speeding ticket (SE).

BLACK AND WHITE CBer: police car with CB (W).

BLACK AND WHITES: police.

BLACK WATER: coffee (SE).

BLEEDING: signal too strong, switch channels (NW); background interrupting transmission (SE).

BLEED OVER: transmission from one channel runs over into another.

BLEW MY DOORS OFF: passed me with great speed; e.g. "'Eh, the Texas Road Runner just blew my doors off."

BLOCKING THE CHANNEL: keying the microphone to prevent messages (SE).

BLOOD BOX: an ambulance.

BLUE AND WHITE: police (MW).

BLUE BOYS: police (SE, SW).

BLUE GRASS STATE: Kentucky.

BLUE JEANS: state troopers (MW).

BLUE LIGHT: marked police car.

BLUE SLIP: speeding ticket (SW).

BOB-TAILING: vehicle without CB following one so equipped.

BODACIOUS: clear reception of signal (SE); e.g. "Mercy sakes, Snow Flake, you're just sounding bodacious out there tonight."

BONE BOX: an ambulance.

BOOB TUBE: television.

BOOGIE MAN: state trooper (NW).

BOOGIEING: nightclubbing.

BOOTLEGGING: using another's CB (W).

BOTH FEET ON THE FLOOR: vehicle is moving at
   fastest possible rate of speed.

BOULEVARD: expressway (SE).

BOUNCE AROUND: return trip (SE); e.g. "See you
   on the bounce around, good buddy."

BOZOS: late night CBers in Nashville, Tennessee
   (SE).

BOX: tractor trailer truck, square and enclosed
   (SE); CB set (SE).

BREAK or BREAK, BREAK: request for use of a
   channel; any attempt to break in between other
   operators.

BREAK FOR *(specific person)*:   call for a specific
   CBer; e.g. "Break for that Cactus Jack just one
   time."

BREAKER *(direction)* BOUND 18:   breaking into a
   channel to talk with any 18 wheeler going in a
   certain direction; e.g. "breaker Westbound 18";
   also, request for police location and road condition report.

BREAKER BROKE: request to use a channel.

BREAKING THE OLD NEEDLE: clear reception of signal (SE).

BREAKING UP: signal is not coming in constantly.

BREAKING WIND: first CB vehicle in a line of two or more (MW).

BRING IT BACK: answer back (SE).

BRING IT ON: answer back; come up here where I am; the way is clear.

BRING YOURSELF ON IN: move into the right lane (SE); answer back (SE).

BROUGHT IT ON: come on up here; the way is clear; answer back.

BROWN BOTTLES: beer.

BROWN PAPER BAG: unmarked police car (NE).

BRUSH YOUR TEETH AND COMB YOUR HAIR: police radar ahead (NW).

B TOWN: Birmingham, Alabama (SE).

BUBBLE TROUBLE: tire ailments.

BUBBLEGUM MACHINE: flashing lights; police.

BUBBLEGUMMER: teenage CBer (W).

BUCKET MOUTH: loud mouth or gossip; obscene or profane talker.

BUCKET OF BOLTS: tractor trailer rig (MW).

BUCKEYE STATE: Ohio.

BUDDY: fellow trucker (SE).

BUFFALO: man; husband.

BUGGERHOLE BUNCH: Irvine, California (W).

BULLET LANE: passing lane (SE); e.g. "Who we got in that Thunder Chicken in the bullet lane?"

BULL JOCKEY: idle talker, one who uses his CB rig to pass the time of day.

BULL RACK: truck hauling animals (NW).

BUMPER LANE: passing lane.

BUTTONPUSHER: one who keys his microphone without speaking, which causes computer inter-ference and humming noise; also prevents messages.

CACTUS JUICE: liquor (SW).

CACTUS PATCH: Phoenix, Arizona; Roswell, New Mexico (SW).

CALLSIGN: official FCC assignment of letters and numbers to a CB operator.

CAMERA: police radar; e.g. "There is a Smokey with a camera at milepost 108."

CANDY MAN: FCC.

CAPITAL J: Jackson, Mississippi (SE).

CASA: home (SW).

CATCH CAR: police car beyond radar set up.

CATCH YOU ON THE OLD FLIP-FLOP: catch you on the radio on a return trip.

CB: Citizens Band radio.

CB LAND: network of CBers.

CHANNEL 11: channel FCC has established as the contact channel after which a user can switch to any other channel that is clear.

CHANNEL 9: emergency channel.

CHANNEL 19: channel truckers use.

CHANNEL 10: channel most truckers east of Kansas City have used in the past.

CHARLIE or CHARLIE, CHARLIE or CHARLIE BROWN: yes.

CHASE CAR: police car guided by a concealed radar unit.

CHECKING MY EYELIDS FOR PIN HOLES: tired, sleepy (W).

CHECK THE SEAT COVERS: look at the passengers, usually women.

CHI TOWN: Chicago, Illinois.

CHICK: woman; girl (NE).

CHICKEN CHOKER: one who masturbates; poultry truck; friendly term truckers use for each other.

CHICKEN COOP: weigh station; e.g. "The chicken coop is clean, bring it on up here."

CHICKEN COOP IS CLEAN: weigh station is closed.

CHOKING THE CHICKEN: masturbation.

CHOO CHOO TOWN: Chattanooga, Tennessee (SE).

CHOPPER IN THE AIR: police helicopter.

CHRISTMAS CARD: speeding ticket (NE).

CIGAR CITY: Tampa, Florida.

CINDERELLA WORLD: Disneyland, California (W).

CIRCLE CITY: Indianapolis, Indiana (MW).

CITY KITTY: local police (MW).

CLASS A STATION: a CB service station licensed to operate from 460 to 470 MHz in the UHF band.

CLASS C STATION: a radio station authorized to transmit controlled signals on specified frequencies in the 26.96 to 27.26 MHz and 72 to 76 MHz bands.

CLASS D STATION: a CB service station licensed to use radio telephony on authorized channels in the 26.96 to 27.26 MHz band. Most CBers have Class D stations.

CLEAN AS A HOUND'S TOOTH: road is clear of police and obstructions (SE).

CLEANER CHANNEL: one freer of interference.

CLEAN SHOT: road is clear of police and obstructions (SE).

CLEAN UP: to be sexually promiscuous (MW); e.g. "I went to Chi Town to clean up, but I ended up choking my chicken."

CLEAR: sign-off; through transmitting.

CLEAR AFTER YOU: after you sign off, the channel will be clear.

CLEAR AND ROLLING: sign-off and moving (SE).

CLEAR AS A SPRING DAY: road is clear of police and obstructions (SE).

CLEAR THERE WITH YOU: sign-off; through transmitting (SE).

CO-AX: coaxial cable.

COCKLEBURR: pep pill (SE).

COFFEEBREAK: small gathering of CBers.

COKE STOP: restroom stop (SW).

COLD COFFEE: beer (SE).

COLLECT CALL: call for a specific CBer.

COLORADO KOOL AID: beer (SW).

COME AGAIN: repeat message.

COME BACK: answer back.

COME HERE: answer back.

COME ON: answer back; e.g. "You got the Shotgun, come on."

COMING IN LOUD AND PROUD: clear reception of signal (SE).

COMING IN TOO TORRIBLE: signal too loud (SE).

COMING OUT OF THE WINDOWS: clear reception of signal (SE).

CONCRETE JUNGLE: expressway (W).

CONVAC: conversation (SE).

CONVOY: a procession of CB vehicles traveling the expressway together, and keeping in constant touch with CBs.

COOKING: driving (SE, MW).

COOKING GOOD: acquired desired speed (MW).

COPY: message; do you understand?; e.g. "Anybody copy this lil' ol' mobile?"

COPYING THE MAIL: monitoring.

CORN BINDER: International Truck (NW).

COTTONPICKER: friendly term truckers use for each other.

COUPON: speeding ticket (SE); e.g. "Mercy sakes, I've already got enough coupons to paper my wall."

COUNTRY CADILLAC: tractor trailer truck (SE).

COUNTRY JOE: rural police (MW).

COUNTY MOUNTY: Sheriff's Department (SE).

COVER: woman; girl (NE).

COVER GROUND: speed up.

COVERED UP: too much interference; I can't understand you; signal isn't clear.

COW TOWN: Ft. Worth, Texas (SE, SW).

CRW: Community Radio Watch.

CRYSTAL: a piece of quartz whose physical dimensions determine the frequency at which it will function as a resonant circuit.

'CUDA: Plymouth Barracuda.

CUP OF MUD: coffee.

CUT LOOSE: sign-off; stop transmitting (SE).

CUT THE CO-AX: turn off the CB set.

DECIBEL (DB): a unit for expression of the ratio of two values, usually power or voltage. It is most often used by CBers in reference to the coaxial cable attenuation loss of antenna gain.

DECOY: unmanned police car.

DEFINITELY: positive intent or agreement.

DELTA TUNE: a control on some CB rigs which permits tuning the receiving frequence slightly off the center to compensate for variations in transmitting frequency of other transceivers.

DERBY CITY: Louisville, Kentucky (MW).

DIARRHEA OF THE MOUTH: talkative (W).

DICE CITY: Las Vegas, Nevada (W).

DIESEL CAR: tractor trailer truck.

DIG YOU OUT: understand you (SE).

DIRT FLOOR: unpaved parking lot.

DIRTY SIDE: New York; New Jersey, the East coast.

DIVORCE CITY: Las Vegas, Nevada (W).

DO IT TO ME: answer back (SE).

DO YOU COPY?: do you understand?

DO YOU HEAR SOMEONE KNOCKING ON YOUR BACK DOOR?: I'm about to pass you.

DOG HOUSE: motor cover on big engine (NW).

DOIN' IT TO IT: full speed (SE); e.g. "We doin' it to it and comin' your way."

DOIN' IT TO IT, THAT WAY: sign-off (SE).

DOING OUR THING IN THE LEFTHAND LANE: full speed in the passing lane; sign-off (SE).

DOING THE FIVE-FIVE: driving at 55 miles per hour; e.g. "The bears are crawling on this ol' super slab today; I been doing the five-five for an hour."

DON'T FEED THE BEARS: don't get a speeding ticket.

DON'T LET YOUR TRICKING TRIP UP YOUR TRUCKING: sign-off (SE).

DON'T LET YOUR TRUCKING TRIP UP YOUR TRICKING: sign-off (SE).

DOT: Canada's Department of Transport, equivalent of FCC.

DOT MAN: Dept. of Transportation representative stopping trucks to check lights, overloads, log books, etc; gives tickets for violations.

DOUBLE BUFFALO: 55 miles per hour.

DOUBLE "L":   telephone.

DOUBLE NICKEL: 55 miles per hour.

DOUBLE NICKEL HIGHWAY: Interstate 55 (SE).

DOUBLE SEVEN: no; negative contact; e.g. "Double seven on that Country Bunny."

DOWN AND GONE: sign-off; turning off CB (SE, MW).

DOWN AND ON THE SIDE: through talking but listening.

DRAGGIN' WAGON;   a wrecker.

DRESS FOR SALE: prostitute (SW).

DRIVING THE PEG: driving the legal speed limit.

DROPPED A CARRIER: keyed the microphone, preventing transmission.

DROPPED IT OFF THE SHOULDER: ran off the side of the highway (SE).

DROP THE HAMMER DOWN: accelerate; no police or obstructions ahead; e.g. "Drop the hammer down and bring it this away."

DUCK PLUCKER: obscene term (euphemism).

DUMMY: unmanned police car; e.g. "Watch for the dummy in the median at milepost 216."

DUSTED MY BRITCHES: passed me (SE, SW).

DUSTED YOUR EARS: transmission interrupted (SE).

D-X: long distance.

EARS: CB radio.

EARS ON: CB radio turned on; e.g. "Got your ears on, good buddy?"

EASTBOUND STRUTTIN' STYLE: headed East at a high rate of speed; sign-off.

EASTBOUND, TRAILER TRUCKIN' STYLE: headed East in a tractor truck; sign-off.

EASY CHAIR: middle CB vehicle in a line of three or more (NW).

EATUM-UP-STOP: roadside restaurant.

EIA: Electronic Industries Association.

EIGHTEEN LEGGED POGO STICK: 18 wheel tractor trailer truck (MW).

EIGHTEEN WHEELER: tractor trailer truck.

EIGHTS AND OTHER GOOD NUMBERS: best wishes; sign-off.

EIGHTY-EIGHTS: love and kisses.

EIGHTY-EIGHTS AROUND THE HOUSE: good luck and best wishes to you and yours.

ELECTRIC TEETH: police radar (SE).

ELEVEN-METER BAND: the 27 MHz citizens band, formerly the eleven-meter amateur band.

E-R-P: effective radiated power. The ERP may be greater or less than the power generated by the transmitter, depending on antenna system gain or loss.

E.R.S.: Emergency Radio Service; Channel 9.

EVERYBODY MUST BE WALKING THE DOG: all channels are busy (SE).

EVERYTHING IS SLICK: the way is clear.

EVEL KNIEVEL SMOKEY: motorcycle police (SW).

EXPRESSWAY BOOGIE: making a long haul trip.

EXTRA MONEY TICKET: speeding ticket (W).

EYEBALL IT: meet; look (SE); e.g. "When that thunder chicken comes 'round ya, eyeball it one time."

EYEBALL TO EYEBALL: two CBers together (SE, SW).

EYE IN THE SKY: police helicopter.

FANCY SEAT COVERS: pretty girls in passing auto.

FAT LOAD: overload, more weight than local state law allows.

FED: inspector, DOT or FCC.

FEED THE BEARS: get caught speeding; e.g. "Don't feed the bears this trip."

FEED THE PONIES OR HORSES: lose money at the horse races (SW).

FIFTY DOLLAR LANE: passing lane (SE).

FINAL: last transmission; e.g. "We'll be clear there with you, on your final."

FINGER WAVE: obscene gesture (SE).

FIRST SERGEANT: wife (W).

FISH: Plymouth Barracuda (SE).

FISHING POLE AND A PARTNER: dual antennas.

FIVE-FIVE: 55 miles per hour.

FIVE WATTS: legal power output for CB set.

FIX: police location report.

FIXED STATION: a radio station at a fixed location.

FLAGWAVER: road construction worker.

FLATBED: tractor trailer truck with flatbed.

FLICK: movie.

FLIGHT MAN: weight station worker on wheels (SE, SW, W).

FLIP or FLIP-FLOP: return trip; e.g. "Enjoyed the modulation, good buddy, catch you on the flip."

FLIP-FLOPPING BEARS: police reversing direction; e.g. "Watch them flip-flopping bears at Exit 143 cuz they be going every which away."

FLIPPER: return trip.

FLOP IT: turn around (SE).

FOLDING CAMERA: the in-car speed monitor in some trooper cars.

FOOT WARMER: linear amplifier.

FORTY-FOURS: children (SW); kisses.

FORTY-ROGER: like 10-4; O.K.; message received, etc.

FORTY WEIGHT: beer (SW).

FOUR: abbreviation of 10-4 meaning yes; O.K., I understand.

FOUR D: yes; O.K. message received; a variation of 10-4.

FOUR LANE PARKING LOT: expressway (W).

FOUR LEGGED BEAST: race horse (W).

FOUR LEGGED GO GO DANCERS: pigs (SE).

FOUR ROGER: message received.

FOUR-TEN: 10-4, emphatically.

FOUR WHEELER: car; small 4 wheel truck.

FOUR WHEELER WITH FIRE IN HIS TAIL: speeding car without CB.

FOX HUNTING: FCC looking for CBers who use profane language or otherwise break FCC regulations; illegal use of CB; e.g. "Uncle Charley's gone fox hunting in Hot Lanta tonight."

FOXY LADY: attractive woman.

FREE RIDE: prostitute (W).

FREQUENCY SYNTHESIZER: a circuit which enables transmit and receive on a number of channels without separate crystals for each function and channel.

FRISCO: San Francisco, California.

FRONT DOOR: first CB vehicle in a line of two or more; e.g. "We got that one Red Pepper running the front door for us."

FRONT DOOR, BACK DOOR, ROCKING CHAIR: the front door and the back door are the road ahead and behind. The lead vehicle in a convoy "watches the front door," the rear watches the back, and those in the middle are "in the rocking chair."

FRONT END: first CB vehicle in a line of two or more (MW).

FULL OF VITAMINS: big engine (SE).

FUNNY BOOKS: pornography.

FUZZ BUSTER: device for detecting radar.

GATEWAY CITY: St. Louis, Missouri (MW).

GEAR JAMMERS: truckers.

GEORGIA OVERDRIVE: neutral gear.

GET HORIZONTAL: sleep; go to bed (W).

GET TRUCKING. make some distance (SE).

GETTING OUT: being heard; clear reception.

GINNING AND GOT THE WHEELS SPINNING: full speed (SE).

GIRLIE BEAR: policewoman (SE).

GIVE ME A SHOT: answer back; call on the CB (SE); e.g. "When you go through that Exit 172, give me a shot. 10-4?"

GIVE ME A SHOUT: answer back; call on the CB (SE).

GO AHEAD: answer back; e.g. "You got the Tennessee Beaver Pleaser, go ahead."

GO BACK TO HIM: talk to him again.

GO BREAKER: permission to speak on channel.

GO BREAK 10: permission to speak on channel.

GO GO GIRLS: load of pigs headed for market.

GO JUICE or GO GO JUICE: gas; fuel.

GO 10-100: restroom stop (W).

GOING-HOME HOLE: high gear.

GONE: through transmitting (SE); e.g. "The one Sugar Britches, KXI-7248, we be gone."

GONE 10-7 PERMANENTLY: deceased.

GOOD BUDDY: salutation originally by truckers but now used by most highway CBers.

GOOD NUMBERS: best wishes; e.g. "We'll be putting the good numbers on you and yours."

GOOD SHOT: road clear of police and obstructions.

GOT A COPY?: do you hear?; e.g. "Anybody got a copy on this One-Eyed Tom, we lookin?"

GOT A 10-2: obtaining a clear reception.

GOT HIS SHOES ON: full speed (SE).

GOT MY EYEBALLS PEELED: I'm looking (SE).

GOT MY FOOT IN IT: accelerating (SE).

GOT YOUR EARS ON?: are you listening?

GRASS: median; e.g. "How about you Eastbound, you got a bear in the grass at Exit 202, 10-4?"

GRASSHOPPER: park policeman.

GREAT BIG SPROCKET: big engine (SE).

GREEN APPLE: a neophyte CBer.

GREEN CBer: military police with CB (W).

GREEN LIGHT: road clear of police and obstructions; e.g. "10-4 guy, you be havin' a green light all the way to that Circle City."

GREEN MACHINE: marine base.

GREEN STAMP COLLECTOR: police radar.

GREEN STAMP LANE: passing lane (SE).

GREEN STAMP ROAD: toll road.

GREEN STAMPS: speeding tickets; money.

GREENS: speeding tickets, money (SE).

GROWED UP TRUCKS: tractor trailers (SE).

CRS: Canadian General Radio Service.

GUITAR TOWN: Nashville, Tennessee (SE, MW).

GUN RUNNER: police radar (SE).

GUTTER BALLING: bowling (W).

GUY: fellow trucker (MW, NE).

H TOWN: Hopkinsville, Kentucky (MW, SE).

HAMBURGER HELPER: linear amplifier (W).

HAMMER: accelerator.

HAMMER DOWN: accelerating; highballing.

HAMMER HANGING: accelerating; same as hammer down.

HAMMER OFF: slow down (NE).

HAMMER ON: accelerating (NE).

HAMMER UP: slow down; police or obstruction ahead.

HANDLE: code name CBer uses in transmission; e.g. "The Stripper;" "Jungle Jim;" "Licketty Split;" "Peanuts;" "Bon Bon;" "Dew Drop."

HANG A RIGHT (or LEFT): turn right or left (MW).

HANG IT IN YOUR EAR: nonsense (W).

HANG MY NEEDLE: receiving strong signal and clear reception.

HANG OUT: monitor a specific channel.

HAPPY NUMBERS: best wishes to you.

HARD ANKLE: working man; trucker.

HARD TO PULL OUT: hard to understand.

HASH AND TRASH: background noise; signal unclear (W).

HAVE A SAFE ONE AND A SOUND ONE: drive safely (SE).

HAVE A 36-24-36 TONIGHT: sign-off.

HAVEN'T SEEN A THING IN YOUR LANE: the way is clear on your side.

HE'S LAYIN', HE'S STAYIN': making the best time possible with the equipment he has; a sign-off.

HIDING IN THE BUSHES, SITTING UNDER THE LEAVES: hidden police car (SE).

HIGH GEAR: use of linear amplifier, an illegal piece of gear which increases output to several hundred watts.

HIND END: last CB vehicle in a line of two or more (SE, SW).

HOG COUNTRY: Arkansas (SE).

HOLE IN THE WALL: tunnel.

HOLLER: a call for a specific person on the CB set; e.g. "Give me a holler next time you're on the ol' channel."

HOME PORT: residence location (SE).

HOME TWENTY: residence location; e.g. "What's your home twenty on that end?"

HONEY WAGON: beer truck (SE).

HORSE: Ford Mustang or Colt (SE, SW); tractor trailer truck (MW).

HOT LANTA: Atlanta, Georgia (SE).

HOT STUFF: coffee (SE).

HOT TOWN: Atlanta, Georgia (SE).

HOT WATER CITY: Hot Springs, Arkansas.

HOW ABOUT *(name)* ONE TIME?: call for a specific CBer (SE); e.g. "How about that Tumbleweed one time?"

HOW ABOUT YOUR VOCAL CORDS? is your set operating? (SE).

HOW AM I HITTING YOU?: how do you receive my transmission?

HOW DO YOU READ ME?: what is the meter reading on my transmission?

HOW TALL ARE YOU?: height of the truck (MW).

HOW WE BE LOOKING BACK YOUR WAY?: is the highway clear the way I'm going?

HUMP: mountain.

HUNDRED MILE COFFEE: strong coffee.

HUSTLER: brand name of antenna; also any antenna.

IF YOU CAN'T USE IT, ABUSE IT: masturbate (MW).

I'M THROUGH: through transmitting.

IN A SHORT, SHORT: soon (SE); e.g. "I'll be back on the rip strip in a short, short."

IN THE GRASS: in the median (SE).

INSTAMATIC: radar set-up.

J TOWN: Jackson, Tennessee (SE).

J TRAIL: CB jamboree season, usually February to November.

JACK IT UP: accelerate (SE); e.g. "Jack it up and brought yourself on up here."

JACK RABBIT: police of any kind (W).

JAMBOREE: large gathering of CBers, often including camp-outs, entertainment, and door prizes.

JIMMIE: a type of tractor trailer truck engine.

JOHN LAW: police of any kind.

K TOWN: Knoxville, Tennessee (SE).

KEEP 'EM BETWEEN THE DITCHES: drive safely (SE).

KEEP THE ROLLING SIDE DOWN AND THE SHINY SIDE UP: drive safely (SE); sign-off.

KEEP THE SHINY SIDE UP AND THE GREASY SIDE DOWN: drive safely (NW); sign-off.

KEEP THE WHEELS SPINNING: drive safely (SE).

KEEP YOUR NOSE BETWEEN THE DITCHES AND SMOKEY OUT OF YOUR BRITCHES: drive safely and look out for speed traps and speeding fines; sign-off.

KEEP YOUR WHEELS OUT OF THE DITCHES AND THE SMOKEYS OUT OF YOUR BRITCHES: drive safely and don't get any speeding tickets; sign-off.

KEEP YOUR WHEELS SPINNING AND THE BEAVERS GRINNING: drive safely and keep the girls happy; sign-off.

KENOSHA CADILLAC: any car made by AMC.

KEYING THE MIKE: activating the microphone without speaking.

KIDDIE CAR: school bus (SE); e.g. "What about that Northbound side, you got a kiddie car at milepost 116; better back 'em on down. 10-4?"

KNOCK IT ABOUT: the way is clear; drive desired speed.

KNOCK THE SLACK OUT: accelerate (SE).

KNOCKING: vehicle moving as best it can.

KNUCKLE BUSTER: fight (W).

KODAK: police radar (SE).

KOJAK: state trooper (SE); e.g. "There's a Kojak with a kodak at Exit 43, better back 'em on down."

KOOL AID: liquor; beer (SE, SW).

LADY BEAR: policewoman.

LADY BREAKER: female CB operator asking for channel.

LAND LINE: telephone.

LAND OF DISNEY: Disneyland, California (W).

LAND OF WONDERFUL: road is clear of police and obstructions (SE).

LATCH-ON: vehicle without CB following one so equipped (SE).

LATRINE LIPS: one who uses profane or obscene language on the CB (W).

LAY AN EYE ON IT: see it.

LAY IT OVER: stand by (SE).

LEFT LANE: passing lane.

LEFT SHOULDER: opposite direction; police situation and road condition; e.g. "Thanks for the come back, good buddy, how's it lookin' over your left shoulder?"

LEGAL BEAGLE: one who uses the correct and legal callsign and abides by FCC rules (W).

LEGALIZED: slowed down to the speed limit; e.g. "Better get legalized, guy, Smokey's ahead at milepost 208."

LET IT GO: drive desired speed (MW).

LET IT ROLL: accelerate; e.g. "The way is clean so let it roll, good buddy."

LET THE CHANNEL ROLL: let others break in and use the channel.

LET THE HAMMER DOWN: full speed; road is clear of police and obstructions.

LETTUCE: money (W).

LET YOUR FLAPS DOWN: slow down (SE).

LID: inept radio operator.

LIGHT FOOTIN' IT: driving the legal speed limit.

LIGHT'S GREEN, BRING ON THE MACHINE: road is clear of police and obstructions; drive at desired speed.

LIL' OL' MODULATOR: CB set.

LINEAR AMPLIFIER: illegal piece of gear which increases output to several hundred watts.

LITTLE BEARS: local police (SE).

LITTLE BIT: prostitute; sexual encounter (SE, MW); e.g. "There's always a little bit at that truck 'em up stop about this time."

LITTLE FOOT WARMER: linear amplifier or power booster.

LOAD OF POSTHOLES: empty truck.

LOAD OF ROCKS: truck hauling bricks (NW).

LOAD OF STICKS: truck hauling cut timber (NW).

LOCAL BEARS: local police.

LOCAL BOY: local police (SE).

LOCAL YOKEL: local police (SE).

LONG DISTANCE TELEPHONE IS RINGING: call for a specific CBer (SE).

L-S-B: lower sideband.

MAGIC CITY: Birmingham, Alabama.

MAGNOLIA STATE: Mississippi (SE).

MAIL: overheard CB conversations; e.g. "I've just been reading the mail tonight."

MAKE A TRIP: switch channels (NW).

MAKE THE TRIP?:   is transmission received?

MAMA: wife (SE).

MAMA SMOKEY: female state trooper (SE).

MAMA'S LANE: passing lane; trucker is anxious to get home to mama (wife).

MAN WITH A GUN: police radar (SE).

MARDI GRAS TOWN: New Orleans, Louisiana.

MARK-L or MARKEL MAN: representative of the Markel Insurance Co. who checks speeding trucks; cannot ticket but can report to company.

MARKER: milepost along expressway; way to determine exact location; e.g. "What's your marker now, good buddy?"

MASHING THE MIKE: keying of the microphone without speaking to prevent messages (SE).

MAY ALL YOUR UPS AND DOWNS BE BETWEEN THE SHEETS: sign-off.

MAYDAY: distress signal.

MEAT WAGON: ambulance (W).

MERCY: universal euphemism for all the naughty words that are illegal on the air.

MERCY SAKES: frequent expression acknowledging reception of remark.

MICKEY MITCHELL: local police (SE).

MICKEY MOUSE METRO ON A TRICYCLE: local police on a three wheel motorcycle (SE).

MIKE: a microphone.

MIK-E-NIK: mechanic, grease monkey (SW).

MILEMARKER: milepost along expressway; method of determining exact location; e.g. "I'm Eastbound on this I-10 at mile marker 186. What's your twenty?"

MILFORD LAND: passing lane.

MINI SKIRT: woman; girl (SE).

MINI STATE: Rhode Island (NE).

MOBILE PARKING LOT: auto carrier (W).

MOBILE UNIT: transceiver installed in a vehicle or carried by a person.

MOBILING: going for a ride (W).

MODULATING: talking; e.g. "Definitely did enjoy modulating with you this mornin' on this ol' base."

MODULATION: talk; voice; conversation.

MODULATION BOOSTER: device or built-in circuit in a CB transceiver which adds gain to a microphone circuit to make it more sensitive, but which automatically limits output to prevent overmodulation.

MONITOR: listen to emergency assistance, Channel 9; listen.

MONKEY TOWN: Montgomery, Alabama (SE).

MONSTER LANE: passing lane (MW).

MOTION-LOTION: gas; fuel (SE); e.g. "I'm peeling off for some of that motion-lotion; see you on the boulevard in a short, short."

MOTOR CITY: Detroit, Michigan.

MOTORING ON: traveling on (SE).

MOUNTIES IN THE SKY: police helicopter (SE).

MOVABLE PARKING DECK: auto carrier.

MOVE: vehicle is in motion.

M20: meeting place (SE).

MUFF: woman; girl.

MUSIC CITY: Nashville, Tennessee (SE).

MUSICAL CITY: Nashville, Tennessee (SE).

MUSKRAT: child (SE, SW).

NASTYVILLE: Nashville, Tennessee (SE).

NCCRA: North Carolina Citizens Radio Association.

NEGATINE: no (SE, SW, W).

NEGATIVE: no.

NEGATIVE COPY: no answer.

NEGATIVE GROUND: the negative battery terminal of a vehicle is connected to the body and frame.

NEGATORY: no.

NIGHTCRAWLERS: police are everywhere (SE).

NINETY WEIGHT: liquor (SW).

NOBODY KNOWS WHERE THE TEDDY BEAR GOES: state troopers are crisscrossing the expressway (SE).

NOISE BLANKER: (See *noise limiter*); similar, but chops holes in the signal path ahead of the detector.

NOISE LIMITER: circuit which reduces impulse type noise in a CB receiver by chopping holes in the audio signal path.

NOTHING BUT A GREEN LIGHT AND A WHITE LINE: the way is clear; sign-off.

O.K.: sign-off.

OLD KITTY WHOMPER: truck (MW).

O-M: old man.

OMNIDIRECTIONAL ANTENNA: an antenna that radiates equally well in all directions.

ON A (*city name*) TURN: return trip from named city (SE); e.g. "I'm on a Memphis turn." (I will make my return from Memphis).

ONE FOOT ON THE FLOOR, ONE HANGING OUT THE DOOR, AND SHE JUST WON'T DO NO MORE: full speed (SE).

ONE HIDING IN THE GRASS: police in the median (SE).

ON SKIP: distant signal.

ON STANDBY: monitoring but not transmitting.

ON THE BY: monitoring but not transmitting.

ON THE MOVE: vehicle is traveling.

ON THE SIDE: standing by and monitoring; parked or pulled over on the shoulder.

OPEN SEASON: police are everywhere (SE).

OPRYLAND: Nashville, Tennessee.

OTHER HALF: wife (usually), or husband.

OTHER RADIO: additional radio to scan police channels (NW).

OUT: through transmitting.

OUTDOOR TV: drive-in movie (W).

OVER: through transmitting but listening.

OVER THE SHOULDER: the road behind, e.g. "Take a peek over your shoulder, good buddy, and tell me about them ol' Smokeys."

OVERMODULATION: talking too long; talking too close to the microphone.

O-W: old woman.

PAIR OF FIVES: 55 miles per hour; the legal speed limit.

PAIR OF NICKELS: 55 miles per hour.

PAIR OF SEVENS: no contact or answer; e.g. "Pair of sevens on that Roving Rebel."

PANIC IN THE STREETS: FCC enforcement apparatus is working the area.

PAPA BEAR: state trooper with CB (MW).

PAPER HANGER: police giving speeding tickets (SE, SW, W).

PAPERWORK: speeding ticket (SE); e.g. "Smokey's got a four wheeler on the side at mile marker 112 and Smokey's doing his paperwork."

PART 15: FCC Rules applicable to the operation of unlicensed radio transmitter.

PART 95: FCC Rules covering CB service.

PASS THE NUMBERS TO YOU: best wishes.

PATCH: city; town.

P.C.: printed circuit.

PAVEMENT PRINCESS: roadside or truckstop prostitute. They have colorful handles like "Bra Buster" and "Panty Stretcher."

PEANUT BUTTER IN HIS EARS: is not listening (SW).

PEDAL AGAINST THE MIDDLE: drive fast (SE).

PEDAL A LITTLE SLOWER: slow down (SE).

PEDAL ALONG WAIT ON YOU: coast (SE).

PEDAL DOWN: drive fast; accelerate.

PEDALING IN THE MIDDLE: straddling both lanes; riding in the middle lane of a three-lane highway (SE); drive fast.

PEELING OFF: getting off the expressway (SE); e.g. "We'll be peeling off the expressway at Exit 202."

PEEL OFF: make the turn (SE).

P-E-P: peak envelope power; the power generated by an SSB transmitter when modulated.

PETER RABBIT: police of any kind (W).

PETRO: gasoline.

PETRO REFINERY: truck hauling gas or oil (SW).

PF FLYERS: truck wheels (SE).

PICK 'EM UP TRUCK: pickup truck.

PICKUM-UP: light truck; pickup truck.

PICKLE SUIT: marine uniform (W).

PICTURE-TAKING MACHINE: police radar.

PIECE OF PAPER: speeding ticket.

PIGEON: vehicle caught speeding (SE); e.g. "The Smokey at milepost 116 has a pigeon."

PIGS: police (W).

PINK PANTHER: unmarked police car; one with CB (SE).

PINK QSL CARD: warning ticket (SW).

PIPE LINE: specific channel; e.g. "We'll give you a holler on the pipe line tomorrow."

PIT STOP: gas stop.

PLAIN BROWN (BLACK, GRAY) WRAPPER: unmarked police car.

POLACK KIDS: cattle (SE).

POLACK SCHOOL BUS: cattle truck (SE).

POLAR BEAR: state trooper.

POLAROID: like picture taker, it connotates radar.

POLE CAT: highway patrol car in black and white (SW).

PORKY BEAR: police of any kind (SE).

PORTABLE BARN YARD: cattle truck.

PORTABLE CAN: long haul tractor trailer carrying liquid; tanker.

PORTABLE FLOOR: flatbed tractor trailer (SE).

PORTABLE GAS STATION: truck transporting gasoline.

PORTABLE PARKING LOT: auto carrier (SE).

PORTABLE PIPELINE: gasoline tank truck; milk tanker.

PORTRAIT PAINTER: police radar (SE).

POSITIVE: yes.

POSITIVE GROUND: the positive battery terminal of a vehicle is connected to the body and frame.

POST: milepost along the expressway.

POTTY MOUTH: one who uses profane or obscene language on the CB (SE).

POUNDS: meter reading in "S" units; e.g. "Thanks for the come back, good buddy. How many pounds am I layin' on you?"

PREGNANT ROLLER SKATE: Volkswagen (W).

PRESS SOME SHEETS: sleep (SW); e.g. "I've been on this rip strip too long; it's time to press some sheets."

P-T-T SWITCH: push-to-talk switch on CB.

PULL IN FOR A SHORT, SHORT: restroom stop (SE).

PULL YOUR HAMMER BACK: slow down; police ahead (SW).

PULLING THE PLUG: turning off the CB set.

PUMPKIN: flat tire. Often results from tire ailments.

PUSHING A RIG: driving a truck.

PUT AN EYEBALL ON HIM: look; saw (SE, SW).

PUT IT ON THE FLOOR AND LOOKING FOR SOME MORE: full speed (SE).

PUT THE GOOD NUMBERS ON YOU: threes and eights; best regards, wishes.

PUT THE WORD ON THE BASE: mobile unit to a base unit which uses telephone (SE).

PUT YOUR FOOT ON THE FLOOR AND LET THE MOTOR TOTER: accelerate (SE).

PUT YOUR PEDAL TO THE MIDDLE AND HAVE YOURSELF A BALL CAUSE IN THAT NORTHBOUND LANE WE HAVEN'T SEEN NOTHIN' AT ALL: the way is clear so drive the desired speed; sign-off.

PUT YOURSELF UP HERE: road is clear of police and obstructions (SE).

PUTTING THE HAMMER DOWN: accelerating.

QSL CARD: postcard bearing callsign of other CB station and used to verify communication or to report reception.

QUASAR: girls; women. Came from Motorola TV commercial, "works in a drawer."

QUEEN CITY: Cincinnati, Ohio (MW).

QUICK TRIP AROUND THE HORN: scanning the 23 CB channels.

RACHET JAWING: talk; idle talk; talking too long.

RADIO CHECK: meter reading; statement of the quality of transmission. Usually asked for by a new CBer who feels left out and wants to use his radio.

RAIN LOCKER: shower room (W).

RAKE THE LEAVES: last CB vehicle in a line of two or more; look for police from the rear.

RALLY: intermediate size CB gathering.

REACT: Radio Emergency Associated Citizens Teams; National Headquarters, 111 East Wacker Drive, Chicago, Illinois, 60601.

REBOUND: return trip (SE); e.g. "Have a good day today and a better day tomorrow and we'll catch you on the rebound."

RED WHEEL: red lights on some police cars (MW).

REEFER: refrigerated truck; e.g. "Reefer full of swinging beefs"—sides of beef on the way to market.

REST: Radio Emergency Safety Teams, organized to monitor radio and citizen's radio service frequencies to aid mariners requiring assistance.

REST 'EM UP PLACE: rest area (SE).

RF: radio frequency.

RIDER: vehicle without CB following one so equipped (SE).

RIG: CB radio and equipment; tractor trailer truck.

RIG RIP-OFF: stolen CB radio.

RIP STRIP: expressway.

RIVER CITY: Memphis, Tennessee (SE); Paducah, Kentucky (MW).

ROAD JOCKEY: driver of tractor trailer.

ROCK: slang for crystal.

ROCK CITY: Little Rock, Arkansas (SE, SW); Chattanooga, Tennessee.

ROCKET CITY: Huntsville, Alabama.

ROCKING CHAIR: middle CB vehicle in a line of three or more.

ROGER: yes; okay; correct.

ROGER ROLLER SKATE: driver doing 20 miles over the speed limit (W); e.g. "There goes a roger roller skate, let him get the bear bite."

ROLLING: moving.

ROLLING BEARS: police on the move (SE).

ROLLING REFINERY: truck hauling gas or oil (SW).

RUBBER CITY: Akron, Ohio (MW).

RUBBER DUCK: lead CB vehicle in a line of two or more. Term came from "Convoy" record.

RUBBERBAND GOING: building speed (SE).

RUBBERNECKERS: lookers; e.g. "The rubber-neckers going past the wreck are causing this four lane parking lot."

RUG RATS: children (W).

RUN INTERFERENCE: speeding car without CB which police will stop.

RUN OUT THE FRONT END: put the backdoor (rear CB vehicle) out of range (SE).

RUNNING BEAR: police on the move.

RUNNING SHOT GUN: driving partner.

RUNNING TOGETHER: CBers staying in contact on the highway (SE).

S AND H GREEN STAMPS: money.

SALT AND PEPPER: police of any kind (MW).

SALT MINES: place of employment.

SAN QUENTIN JAIL BAIT: underage female hitch-hitcher (SE).

SCAB: term ham operators use for CBers.

SCALE HOUSE: weigh station; e.g. "Bring yourself on up here, the scale house is clean."

SCALE HOUSE IS ALL RIGHT: weigh station is closed.

SCANNER RECEIVER: one that automatically tunes itself to preselected channels, stopping where a signal is heard and resuming scanning when signal is gone.

SCATTERSTICK: vertical antenna with a ground plane.

SCHOOL TWENTY: location of school.

SCOFFLAW: FCC rule violator.

SCRATCHIN': vehicle is moving at its best pace.

SEAT COVER: attractive woman or girl; passenger; e.g. "Hey, good buddy, lay an eyeball on that seat cover comin' up in that show-off lane."

SET OF DOUBLES: tractor trailer truck.

SEVENTY-THIRDS TO YOU: sign-off; best wishes.

SEVENTY-THREE: best wishes.

SHAKE THE BUSHES: lead CB vehicle looking for police, obstructions (NW).

SHAKE THE LEAVES: lead CB vehicle looking for police, obstructions.

SHAKE THE TREES: same as "shake the leaves."

SHAKEY CITY: Los Angeles, California.

SHAKING IT: moving (SE).

SHAKING THE WINDOWS: clear reception of signal (W).

SHANTY SHAKER: truck delivering mobile homes.

SHOES: linear amplifiers; illegal piece of gear which increases output to several hundred watts.

SHORT, SHORT: soon; restroom stop.

SHOT AN EYEBALL ON IT: saw it (MW).

SHOT GUN: police radar gun; e.g. "How about it I-40, we definitely got a bear with a shot gun at Exit 31."

SHOUT: call for a specific person on the CB set; e.g. "I'm hanging out on channel 13 now, give me a shout tonight."

SHOVELLING COAL: accelerating (SE).

SHOW-OFF LANE: passing lane (SE).

SIDEDOOR: passing lane (SE); e.g. "Who we got comin' up on my sidedoor?"

SIN CITY: Cincinnati, Ohio (MW); Las Vegas, Nevada (W).

SITTING IN THE SADDLE: middle CB vehicle in a line of three or more (SE).

SIX WHEELER: small truck; passenger car pulling a trailer.

SKIP: radio signal from a distant radio station reflected by the ionosphere.

SKIPLAND: distant radio signal.

SKIPPERS: CBers who talk on long range signal.

SKIP SHOOTER: unlicensed CBer (NW).

SKIPTALK: long range signal creating congestion for local CBers; activity of talking with distant CBers.

SKY BEAR: police helicopter.

SKY MOUNTY: police helicopter.

SLAMMER: jail (W).

SLIDER: between the channels, as on a sideband radio (NW).

SLOP: bad fuel (SE).

SLOPPY JOES: state troopers (SE).

"S" METER: meter which indicates the level of an intercepted signal and which is calibrated in "S" units. One "S" unit equals 5 decibels (DB). (CBers refer to "S" units as *pounds*.)

> 1 "S" unit = faint, barely perceptible
> 2 "S" units = very weak signal
> 3 "S" units = weak signal
> 4 "S" units = fair signal
> 5 "S" units = fairly good signal
> 6 "S" units = good signal
> 7 "S" units = moderately strong signal
> 8 "S" units = strong signal
> 9 "S" units = extremely strong signal

SMILE AND COMB YOUR HAIR: radar ahead (SE, SW): e.g. "Better smile and comb your hair when you go by that mile marker 186."

SMOKE 'EM UP BEAR: police of any kind (SE).

SMOKE ON BROTHER: accelerate (SE).

SMOKE (SMOKEY) REPORT: police location report.

SMOKE SCREEN: police radar (SE).

SMOKE SOME DOPE: accelerate (SE); e.g. "You got the green light so smoke some dope if you want to."

SMOKEY: police of any kind.

SMOKEY BEAVER: policewoman (SE).

SMOKEY DOZING: patrol car stopped.

SMOKEY ON FOUR LEGS: mounted police (used in New York City and Chicago only).

SMOKEY ON RUBBER: policeman moving.

SMOKEY ON THE GROUND: policeman out of the patrol car.

SMOKEY TWO WHEELER: motorcycle cop (W).

SMOKEY WITH A CAMERA: police with radar.

SMOKEY WITH EARS: police with CB set; e.g. "Talk to the Pig Iron; he's a Smokey with ears."

SMOKEY'S THICK: police are everywhere (NE).

SNAFU: foul up.

SNAKE DEN: fire station (SW).

SNEAKY SNAKE: hidden patrol car; police with CB set (SE); e.g. "How about you 18 wheelers on this I-55; we got a sneaky snake on the overpass at Exit 22. 10-4?"

SNOOPERS: lights on a marked police car; e.g. "Here comes a Tijuana taxi with its snoopers on."

SNUFF-DIPPERS: roadside or truckstop prostitutes.

SOLID STATE: electronic device or circuit employing no tubes.

SOMEONE SPILLED HONEY ON THE ROAD: state troopers ahead everywhere (NW).

SOUNDING CHOICE: clear reception of signal.

SPARKIE: electrician (W).

SPOKE TO US: answer back (SE); e.g. "Come on, you got that one and only Sugar Britches, spoke to us."

SPORT CITY: Shreveport, Louisana (SE).

SPREADING THE GREENS: police passing out speeding tickets (SE).

SPY IN THE SKY: police helicopter (SE); e.g. "We got a spy in the sky at this Exit 182 on this I-40."

SQUELCH: electronic circuit in a receiver which mutes the speaker except when a radio signal is intercepted; cuts out noise between intercepted transmissions.

S|rf METER: provided on some CB rigs to indicate relative strength of an intercepted signal when receiving and the relative rf power output when transmitting.

SSB: single sideband. An AM radio transmission technique in which only one sideband is transmitted. The other one and the carrier are suppressed.

STACK THEM EIGHTS: best regards.

STAGE STOP: truck stop (SW).

STATE BEAR: state trooper.

STATION LICENSE: in the Citizens Radio Service, a license granted by the FCC to operate any number of transceivers under control of the same license.

STAY BETWEEN THE JUMPS AND BUMPS: drive safely; sign-off.

STEPPED ALL OVER YOU: interrupted transmission (SE).

STEPPED ON THE BEAR'S TOES: broke the law, speed limit, etc. (SE).

STEPPING: moving (SE).

STOP TO GET GROCERIES: stop and eat (SW).

STRAIGHT SHOT: road is clear of police and obstructions (SE); e.g. "You definitely got a straight shot all the way in to that Shakey City. Come on!"

STREAKING: full speed (MW); e.g. "Mercy sakes we be doin' it to it in the left lane and we be definitely streaking."

STUPEN: pretending (SE); e.g. "That bear's not stupen; he's passin' out those green stamps."

SUDS: beer (W).

SUPER CHICKENS: trucks belonging to Yellow Freight System.

SUPER SKIRT: girl or woman.

SUPERDOME CITY: New Orleans, Louisiana (SE).

SUPER SLAB: expressway.

SUPPOSITORY: negative; no (SE).

SWEEPING LEAVES: bringing up the rear. See also "back door" and "raking the leaves."

SWEET THING: female CB operator.

SWINDLE SHEET: trucker's log sheet.

SWR: standing wave ratio.

SWR METER: a circuit which measures the standing wave ratio at the transceiver end of the antenna transmission line.

SYNTHESIZER: device for crystal controlling a large number of frequencies with a few crystals.

T-R SWITCH: transmit-receive switch.

T TOWN: Texarkana, Texas and Arkansas (SW).

TAKING PICTURES: police radar; e.g. "You got a bear in the median at Exit 204 and he's taking pictures for sure. 10-4?"

TAKING PICTURES EACH WAY: two-way police radar.

TANKER: tractor trailer carrying liquid.

TAXI: marked police car; short for Tijuana taxi.

TEN-CODE: abbreviations originally used by police and other land mobiles, now widely used by CBers; used to minimize the use of air time.

TEN-CODE (OFFICIAL):

10-1	Receiving poorly
10-2	Receiving well
10-3	Stop transmitting
10-4	OK, message received
10-5	Relay message

TEN-CODE (OFFICIAL)—CONTINUED:

10-6	Busy, stand by
10-7	Out of service, leaving air
10-8	Inservice, subject to call
10-9	Repeat message
10-10	Transmission complete, standing by
10-11	Talking too rapidly
10-12	Visitors present
10-13	Advise weather and road condition
10-16	Make pickup at_____
10-17	Urgent business
10-18	Anything for us?
10-19	Nothing for you, return to base
10-20	My location is_____
10-21	Call by telephone
10-22	Report in person to_____
10-23	Stand by
10-24	Completed last assignment
10-25	Can you contact_____?
10-26	Disregard last message
10-27	I am moving to channel____
10-28	Identify your station
10-29	Time is up for contact
10-30	Does not conform to FCC rules
10-32	I will give you a radio check
10-33	EMERGENCY TRAFFIC AT THIS STATION
10-34	TROUBLE AT THIS STATION, NEED HELP
10-35	Confidential information
10-36	Correct time is_____
10-37	Wrecker needed at_____
10-38	Ambulance needed at_____
10-39	Your message delivered
10-41	Please tune to channel____
10-42	Traffic accident at_____

TEN-CODE (OFFICIAL)—CONTINUED:

10-43	Traffic tieup at_____
10-44	I have a message for you
10-45	All units within range please report
10-46	Assist motorist
10-50	Break channel
10-60	What is next message number?
10-62	Unable to copy; use phone
10-63	Network directed to_____
10-64	Network clear
10-65	Awaiting your next message/assignment
10-67	All units comply
10-69	Message received
10-70	Fire at_____
10-71	Proceed with transmission in sequence
10-73	Speed trap at_____
10-74	Negative
10-75	You are causing interference
10-77	Negative contact
10-81	Reserve hotel room for_____
10-82	Reserve room for_____
10-84	My telephone number is_____
10-85	My address is_____
10-89	Radio repairman needed at_____
10-90	I have T.V.I.
10-91	Talk closer to the mike
10-92	Your transmission is out of adjustment
10-93	Check my frequency on this channel
10-94	Please give me a long count
10-95	Transmit dead carrier for five seconds
10-97	Check test signal
10-99	Mission completed, all units secure
10-200	Police needed at_____

TEN-CODE (ABBREVIATED): abbreviated code recommended for CB users:

10-1	Signal weak
10-2	Signal good
10-3	Stop transmitting
10-4	Affirmative, ok
10-5	Relay to_____
10-6	Busy
10-7	Out of service
10-8	In service
10-9	Repeat
10-10	Negative
10-11	On duty
10-12	Stand by (stop)
10-13	Existing conditions
10-14	Message/information
10-15	Message delivered
10-16	Reply to message
10-17	Enroute
10-18	Urgent
10-19	(In) contact
10-20	Location
10-21	Call_____by phone
10-22	Disregard
10-23	Arrived at scene
10-24	Assignment completed
10-25	Report to meet
10-26	Estimated arrival time
10-27	License/permit information
10-28	Ownership information
10-29	Records check
10-30	Danger/caution
10-31	Pickup

TEN-CODE (ABBREVIATED)—CONTINUED:

10-32	Units needed
10-33	Help me quickly
10-34	Time

TEN-FOUR: hello; positive; yes; O.K.; I understand; do you understand?; what?; definitely; e.g. "A big ten-four to that, good buddy." Ten-four is the most widely and frequently used term in CB slanguage.

TEN ONE HUNDRED (10-100): restroom stop (SW, W).

TEN ONE THOUSAND (10-1000): FCC rep. (W).

TEN ROGER: message received.

TEN-TEN AND LISTNIN' IN: transmission is complete and I'm monitoring.

TEN-TEN 'TIL WE DO IT AGAIN: sign-off.

TEN TWO THOUSAND (10-2000): dope pusher (W).

TENNESSEE SLICK STICKS: Nuetronics Hustler Phased Antennas; dual antennas.

TENNIS SHOES: truck tires.

TEXAS STRAWBERRIES: shelled corn (SW).

THERMOS BOTTLE: milk tanker; gasoline tank truck.

THIRTY WEIGHT: coffee (SW).

THREE LEGGED BEAVER: male homosexual.

THREES: short for 73s, which is a salutation; it can mean hello or goodbye; e.g. "I'll say threes, Sugar Britches."

THREES AND EIGHTS: sign-off; best wishes (SW).

THREES ON YOU: best regards.

THUNDER CHICKEN: Ford Thunderbird (SE).

TIGHTEN UP ON THE RUBBERBAND: accelerate (SE).

TIGHTEN YOUR SEAT DOWN, WE'RE RUNNING HEAVY: we are accelerating (SE).

TIJUANA TAXI: police; wrecker (MW); car bristling lights and markings.

TINSEL CITY: Hollywood, California (W).

TOENAILS ARE SCRATCHING: full speed (SE).

TOENAILS IN THE RADIATOR: full speed (SE).

TOENAILS ON THE FRONT BUMPER: full speed (SE).

TOILET MOUTH: one who uses profane or obscene language on the CB (W).

TOP TWENTY: national CB jamboree held three days each year in a different city.

TRADING STAMPS: money; e.g. "I got a pocket full of trading stamps and I'm free to spend 'em."

TRAILER TRUCKING: 18 wheeler's term for driving his rig.

TRAIN STATION: traffic court that fines everybody.

TRANSCEIVER: combination radio transmitter and receiver.

TRANSMISSION LINE: the coaxial cable that is used to connect the transceiver to the antenna on CB rigs.

TRICK BABE: prostitute (SW).

TRICKY DICK'S: San Clemente, California (W).

TRUCK 'EM EASY: drive safely; e.g. "You truck 'em easy now and don't let those Smokeys get in your britches."

TRUCK 'EM UP STOP: truck stop.

TRUCKIN' GUY: fellow truck driver (NE, MW).

TURKEY: dumb (W).

TURNING MY HOUSE AROUND: turning the antenna for better reception (W).

TURN OVER: stop; e.g. "We'll turn over at that Exit 204."

TURN TWENTY: location of exit or turn.

T-V-I: television interference from CB sets.

TWELVES: company present (SW).

TWENTY: location; e.g. "What's your twenty now, good buddy?"

TWIN HUSKIES: dual antenna (SE, SW, W).

TWO MILES OF DITCHES FOR EVERY MILE OF ROAD: drive safely; keep rig in the middle (MW); sign-off.

TWO-WHEELERS: motorcycles.

T-X: telephone

UCBTA: United CB Truckers Association, P.O. Box 2676, Garland, Texas, 75041.

UNCLE CHARLEY: FCC; e.g. "Uncle Charley has gone fox hunting in that Circle City tonight."

UNIT: one of the transceivers covered by a CB station license when more than one transceiver is used.

U-S-B: upper sideband.

USCRC: United States Citizens Radio Council, 3600 Noble, Anniston, Alabama 36201.

USE THE JAKE: slow down (SW); e.g. "You 18 wheelers on that Eastbound side better use the jake, we've got some slick spots through here."

VAN: tractor trailer truck.

VOX: voice operated relay, alternate to "push to talk" button on the mike, used to activate the transmit circuitry to transmitters.

WALKIE-TALKIE: portable transceiver.

WALKING IN HERE BLOWING SMOKE: clear reception of signal (SE).

WALKING ON YOU: covering up your signal; e.g. "Come back on that, guy, they're walking on you."

WALKING THE DOG: clear reception of signal.

WALL TO WALL BEARS: police are everywhere; radar set-up or road block (NE).

WALL TO WALL AND TREE TOP TALL: clear reception of signal (W).

WALL TO WALL, TEN FEET TALL: clear reception of signal (SE).

WALLPAPER: QSL card (NW).

WARDEN: wife.

WATCH THE PAVEMENT: drive safely (SE).

WATCH YOUR DONKEY: police coming up from behind (NW); e.g. "You shake the leaves, and I'll watch your donkey for you."

WATER HOLE: truck stop (SW).

WATERGATE TOWN: Washington, D.C.

WAY IS BUENO: road is clear of police and obstructions (SW).

WE BE TOPPIN' THESE HILLS AND POPPIN' THESE PILLS: truckers' sign-off.

WE GO: through transmitting, a sign-off.

WE GONE: stopping our sending; we'll listen.

WE UP, WE DOWN, WE CLEAR, WE GONE: sign-off.

WE WENT: sign-off.

WEEKEND WARRIORS: National Guard.

WEIGHT WATCHER: weigh station worker (W).

WELFARE STATION: CB purchased with welfare money (W).

WE'LL BE DOIN' IT THE OTHER WAY: we're headed in the opposite direction from you.

WE'RE BACKING 'EM UP NOW: sign-off; slow down (SE).

WE'RE CLEAR: sign-off; road is clear of police and obstructions; e.g. "The one Sugar Britches, KXI-7248, we're clear."

WE'RE DOWN: sign-off (SE).

WE'RE DOWN, OUT, ON THE SIDE: through transmitting but listening (SE).

WE'RE LISTENING: answer back (SE); e.g. "What about that Triple Six one time, we're listening."

WE'RE LOOKING: answer back (SE).

WE'RE OUT: clear of police and obstructions; sign-off.

WE'RE OUT OF IT: clear of police and obstructions; sign-off.

WE'RE TRYING: distant attempt for CB contact.

WEST BOUND AND LOOKIN' AROUND: sign-off.

WHAT AM I PUTTING ON YOU?: request for meter reading; desire to know signal strength.

WHAT ARE YOU PUSHING?: what are you driving?

WHATEVERS: state troopers.

WHAT KIND OF COPY?: request for meter reading; desire to know strength and clarity of signal.

WHAT'S YOUR EIGHTEEN?: what kind of truck are you driving?

WHAT'S YOUR TWENTY?: request for location.

WHEN DID YOU GET IN THIS BUSINESS?: how long have you had a CB? (SE).

WHERE DO YOU GET YOUR GREEN STAMPS?: where do you work?

WHIMP: man with little personality or courage (NW).

WHITE KNIGHT: state trooper; came from record by same title.

WHO DO YOU PULL FOR?: who do you work for? (SE).

WHOMPING ON YOU: interrupting transmission (SE); e.g. "Come back on that, good buddy, somebody's whomping on you."

WILCO: I will comply.

WINDY CITY: Chicago, Illinois.

WOOD BUTCHER: carpenter (W).

WOOLY BEAR: woman (SE).

WOOLY-WOOLY: woman (SE).

WORKING MAN: truck driver (MW).

WORK TWENTY: place of employment.

WRAP IT UP AND TAKE IT BACK: after your sign-off, we'll be through talking.

WRAPPER: unmarked police car; e.g. "Eh there on that Southbound side, you've got a white wrapper in your lane at mile post 269. 10-4?"

WRINKLE: uneven transmission (SE).

X-L: unmarried woman (W).

X-RAY MACHINE: police radar; e.g. "Smokey's got his X-ray machine working at Exit 15."

X-RAYING: trooper with radar.

X-Y: spouse.

X-Y-D: daughter.

X-Y-L: wife (stands for ex-young lady).

X-Y-M: husband.

X-Y-N: male (SW).

X-Y-O: spouse (NW).

YAP: conversation on CB.

YELLOWSTONE PARK: congregation of state troopers; road block or radar with several chase cars (NW, SE).

Y-L: young lady.

YO: yes (SE).

YOU GOT IT: answer back (MW).

YOU'RE LOOKING GOOD: clear reception of signal (SE).

YOUR TELEPHONE IS RINGING: call for specific CBer (SE); e.g. "How about that, Mr. McGoo one time. Your telephone is ringing."

YO YO: vehicle varying speed (SE).

ZAPPING: overload from a passing vehicle using a powerful linear amplifier at close range, damaging the receiver section of a CB.

CROSS-REFERENCE

ACCELERATE
both feet on the floor
cover ground
get trucking
hammer down
hammer hanging
hammer on
jack it up (SE)
kick the slack out (SE)
let it go
let it roll

ACCELERATE—CONTINUED:
> pedal against the middle (SE)
> pedal down
> put the hammer down
> put your foot on the floor and let the motor toter (SE)
> rubberband going
> shovel coal (SE)
> smoke on brother (SE)
> smoke some dope (SE)
> tighten up on the rubberband

ACCELERATOR
> hammer

ACTIVATING THE MIKE WITHOUT SPEAKING
> buttonpushing
> dropping a carrier
> keying the mike
> mashing the mike (SE)

AKRON, OHIO
> Rubber City (MW)

ALL CHANNELS ARE BUSY
> everybody must be walking the dog (SE)

AMARILLO, TEXAS
> Big A (SW)

AMBULANCE
> blood box
> bone box
> emergency vehicle
> meat wagon (W)

AMC CAR
Kenosha Cadillac

ANSWER BACK
back
back at you
back to you
bring it on
bring it back (SE)
bring yourself on in (SE)
come back
come here
come on
do it to me (SE)
give me a shot (SE)
give me a shout
go ahead
go back to him
go breaker
how about your vocal cords
how am I hitting you
spoke at us (SE)
we're listening (SE)
we're looking (SE)
you got it (MW)

ANTENNA
fishing pole and a partner
beam
hustler
Tennessee slick sticks
twin huskies (SW, SE, W)

ARKANSAS
hog country (SE)

ATLANTA, GEORGIA
  Hot Lanta (SE)
  Hot Town (SE)

ATTRACTIVE WOMAN
  foxy lady
  seat cover

AUTO CARRIER
  mobile parking lot (W)
  movable parking deck
  portable parking lot (SE)

BACKGROUND NOISE
  background too heavy (SE)
  hash and trash (W)

BAD FUEL
  slop (SE)

BATON ROUGE, LOUISIANA
  B. R. Town

BEER
  barley pop (NW)
  brown bottle
  cold coffee (SE)
  Colorado Kool aid (W)
  Kool aid (SE)
  forty weight (SW)
  honey (SE)
  suds (W)

BEER TRUCK
  honey wagon

BEST WISHES
  eights and other good numbers
  eighty-eights around the house
  good numbers
  happy numbers
  pass the numbers to you
  seventy thirds
  stack them eights
  threes
  threes and eights (SW)
  threes on you

BIG ENGINE
  full of vitamins (SE)
  great big sprocket (SE)

BIRMINGHAM, ALABAMA
  B Town (SE)
  Magic City

BOSTON, MASSACHUSETTS
  Bean Town

CALL CHANNEL
  Channel 11

CALL FOR SPECIFIC CBer
  break for *(handle)*
  collect call
  holler
  how about *(handle)*
  long distance telephone
  shout

CAR
  four wheeler
  mobile

CARPENTER
  wood butcher (W)

CATTLE
  Polack kids (SE)

CATTLE TRUCK
  Polack school bus (SE)
  portable barnyard

CB GATHERING
  coffeebreak
  jamboree
  rally

CB NETWORK
  CB Land

CB RADIO AND EQUIPMENT
  box (SE)
  ears
  lil' ol' modulator
  rig
  set
  vocal cords

CHANNEL
  pipeline

CHANNEL 1
  basement (NW)

CHATTANOOGA, TENNESSEE
  Choo Choo Town (SE)
  Rock City

CHICAGO, ILLINOIS
Windy City
Chi Town

CHILDREN
forty-fours (SW)
muskrats (SE) (SW)
rug rats (W)

CINCINNATI, OHIO
Queen City (MW)
Sin City (MW)

CITY OR TOWN
patch

CLEAR RECEPTION
bending the windows (SE)
big ears
bodacious (SE, SW)
breaking the old needle (SE)
coming in loud and proud (SE)
coming out the windows (SE)
dig you out
getting out
got a 10-2
hang my needle
make the trip
pull you out
shaking the windows (W)
sounding choice
walking in here blowing smoke
walking the dog
wall to wall, ten feet tall (SE)
you're looking good (SE)

COAST
  pedal
  pedal along and wait on me (SE)

COAXIAL CABLE
  co-ax
  transmission line

CODE NAME OF CBer
  handle

COFFEE
  black water (SE)
  cup of mud
  hot stuff (SE)
  thirty weight (SW)

COMPANY PRESENT
  twelves (SW)

CONVERSATION
  convac (SE)
  modulating
  rachet jawing
  yap

CRYSTAL
  rock

DALLAS, TEXAS
  Big D (SW)

DAUGHTER
  X-Y-D

DEAD PERSON
   gone 10-7 permanently

DEPARTMENT OF TRANSPORTATION REPRE-
   SENTATIVE
   DOT man

DESIRED SPEED
   cooking good
   letting it go
   motor is totering

DETROIT, MICHIGAN
   Motor City

DEVICE FOR DETECTING RADAR
   fuzz buster

DIRECTIONAL ANTENNA
   beam

DISNEYLAND, CALIFORNIA
   Cinderella World (W)
   Land of Disney (W)

DISTANT RADIO SIGNAL
   on skip
   skip
   skipland
   skiptalk

DISTRESS SIGNAL
   Mayday
   10-34 (official)
   10-33 (abbreviated)

DOPE PUSHER
   10-2000 (W)

DO YOU HEAR ME?
   do you copy?
   how about your vocal cords?
   how do you read me?
   make the trip?
   what am I putting on you?

DRIVE-IN MOVIE
   outdoor tv (W)

DRIVE SAFELY
   have a safe one and a sound one (SE)
   keep 'em between the ditches (SE)
   keep the rolling side down and the shiny side up
      (SE)
   keep the shiny side up and the greasy side
      down (NW)
   keep the wheels spinning (SE)
   stay between the jumps and the bumps
   truck 'em easy
   two miles of ditches for every mile of road, keep
      your rig in the middle (MW)
   watch the pavement (SE)

DRIVING
   cooking (SE)
   pushing a rig

DRIVING PARTNER
   running shot gun

EATING STOP
   stop to get groceries (W)
   eatum-up stop

ELECTRICIAN
   sparkie (W)

EMERGENCY CHANNEL
   Channel 9

EMPTY POLICE CAR
   decoy
   dummy

EMPTY TRUCK
   load of postholes

EXPRESSWAY
   big slab
   boulevard (SE)
   concrete jungle (W)
   four lane parking lot (W)
   rip strip
   super slab

FCC
   candy man
   fed
   fox hunter
   panic in the streets
   10-1000 (W)
   Uncle Charley

FCC RULE VIOLATOR
   scofflaw

FIFTY-FIVE MILES PER HOUR
   doing the five-five
   double nickle

FIFTY-FIVE MILES PER HOUR—CON'T.
driving the peg
double buffalo
legalized
light footin' it
pair of fives
pair of nickels

FIGHT
knuckle buster (W)

FIRE STATION
snake den (SW)

FIRST CBer IN A LINE
beat the bushes
clearing the way
front door
front end (MW)
rubber duck
shake the bushes
shake the leaves
shake the trees

FLASHING LIGHTS
advertising
bubblegum machine
red wheel (MW)

FLATBED TRACTOR TRAILER
portable floor (SE)

FLORIDA
Bikini State

FORD MUSTANG OR COLT
 horse (SE, SW)

FORD THUNDERBIRD
 bird
 Thunder Chicken (SE)

FORREST CITY, ARKANSAS
 Bar City (SE)

FOUL UP
 snafu

FREE CHANNEL
 cleaner channel

FT. WORTH, TEXAS
 Cow Town (SE, SW)

FULL SPEED
 doing our thing in the lefthand lane (SE)
 doin' it to it (SE)
 drop the hammer down
 ginning and got the wheels spinning (SE)
 got his shoes on (SE)
 got my foot on it (SE)
 hammer on (NE)
 let it go
 let the hammer down
 light's green, bring on the machine
 motor on
 one foot on the floor, one hanging out the door
  and she just won't do anymore (SE)
 put it on the floor and looking for some more
  (SE)

FULL SPEED—CONTINUED
rubberband going
streaking (MW)
tighten up on the rubberband (SE)
tighten your seat down (SE)
toenails in the radiator (SE)
toenails on the bumper (SE)

GAS OR FUEL
go juice
go go juice
motion-lotion (SE)
petro

GAS STOP
pit stop

GIRL
beaver (SE)
chick (NE)
cover (NE)
fancy seat cover
foxy lady
lady breaker
mini skirt (SE)
muff
quasar
seat cover
skirt
super skirt
sweet thing
wooly bear (SE)
wooly-wooly (SE)

GREYHOUND BUS
big dog

HAM RADIO OPERATORS TERM FOR CBer
  scab

HIDDEN PATROL CAR
  dummy
  hiding in the bushes (SE)
  pink panther (SE, SW)
  sitting under the leaves
  sneaky snake (SE)

HIGH GEAR
  going home gear

HOLLYWOOD, CALIFORNIA
  Tinsel City (W)

HOME
  home twenty
  casa (SW)

HOPKINSVILLE, KENTUCKY
  H town (SE, SW)

HOT SPRINGS, ARKANSAS
  Hot Water City

HOUSTON, TEXAS
  Astrodome City (SE)

HUNTSVILLE, ALABAMA
  Rocket City

HUSBAND
  buffalo
  other half
  X-Y-M

IDLE TALKER
bull jockey
rachet jawer

ILLEGAL USE OF CB
apple
fox hunting
skip shooting (NW)

INDIANAPOLIS, INDIANA
Circle City (NW)

INEPT RADIO OPERATOR
green apple
lid

INITIAL TRANSMISSION
break
break, break
break channel (nos.)
 callsign (FCC)
breaker broke
break for *(specific name)*
break 10
give me a shot
how about a *(direction)* bound
how about you *(name)*
what about that *(name)*

INTERNATIONAL TRUCK
corn binder (NW)

INTERRUPTED TRANSMISSION
bleeding (SE)
breaking up
covered up

INTERRUPTED TRANSMISSION—CON'T.
    dusted your ears (SE)
    walking on you (SE)
    whomping on you (SE)

INTERSTATE 55
    double nickel highway (SE)

IRVINE, CALIFORNIA
    Bugger Hole Bunch (W)

JACKSON, MISSISSIPPI
    Capital J

JACKSON, TENNESSEE
    J Town (SE)

JAIL
    slammer (W)

JAMBOREE SEASON
    J Trail

KENTUCKY
    Blue Grass State

KEYING THE MIKE TO PREVENT MESSAGES
    blocking the channel (SE)
    buttonpushing
    dropped a carrier on us
    mashing the mike (SE)

KISSES
    forty-fours

KNOXVILLE, TENNESSEE
    K Town (SE)

LAS VEGAS, NEVADA
    Dice City (W)
    Divorce City (W)
    Sin City (SW, W)

LAW ENFORCEMENT:
    (GENERAL)
    bear
    bearded buddy (SE)
    big brother
    black and white
    blue and white (MW)
    bubblegum machine
    camera
    catch car
    chase car
    electric teeth (SE)
    Evel Knievel smokey (SW)
    girlie bear
    grasshopper
    green stamp collector
    gun runner (SE)
    Jack Rabbit (W)
    John Law
    lady bear
    nightcrawlers (SE)
    open season (SE)
    papa bear (MW)
    paperhanger (SE, SW, W)
    Peter Rabbit (W)
    picture taking machine
    pigs (W)
    plain wrapper
    porky bear (SE)
    red wheel (MW)

LAW ENFORCEMENT (GEN.):—CON'T.

running bear
salt and pepper (MW)
shot gun
smoke 'em up bear (SE)
smoke report
smoke screen (SE)
smokey
smokey beaver (SE, SW, W)
smokey on four legs
smokey's thick (NE)
sneaky snake (SE)
Tijuana taxi
wall to wall bears (SE, SW, W)
x-ray machine

(LOCAL POLICE)
blue boy (SE)
city kitty (MW)
country joe (MW)
little bear (SE)
local bear
local boy (SE)
local yokel (SE)
mickey mitchell (SE)
mickey mouse metro on a tricycle (SE)
smokey on four legs
smokey two wheeler

(STATE TROOPER)
barnie (SW)
blue jeans (MW)
boogie man (NW)
Kojak
pink panther (SE, SW)

LAW ENFORCEMENT (ST. TRP.)—CON'T.

polar bear
pole cat (SW)
sloppy joe
someone spilled honey on the road (NW)
state bear
whatevers
white knight
Yellowstone Park

(SHERIFF'S DEPARTMENT)
county mounty
mounty

LAW ENFORCEMENT WITH CB

black and white CBer (W)
papa bear (MW)
smokey with ears
sneaky snake (SE)

LEGAL USE OF CB

legal beagle (W)

LEGAL OPERATION OF CB

barefoot
barefoot mobile

LINEAR AMPLIFIER

foot warmer
hamburger helper (W)
high gear
shoes

LIQUOR

cactus juice (SW)
Kool aid
ninety weight (SW)

LITTLE ROCK, ARKANSAS
  Rock City (SE, SW)

LOCATION
  10-20
  twenty

LOCATION OF EMPLOYMENT
  where do you get your green stamps?
  who do you pull for? (SE)
  work twenty

LOCATION OF SCHOOL
  school twenty

LOCATION OF TURNOFF
  turn twenty

LONG DISTANCE
  D-X

LOOK
  check the seat covers
  put an eyeball on it (SE, SW)

LOOKERS
  rubberneckers

LOS ANGELES, CALIFORNIA
  Shakey City

LOSE MONEY AT THE HORSE RACES
  feed the ponies (SW)

LOUD MOUTH OR GOSSIP
  bucket mouth

LOUISVILLE, KENTUCKY
Derby City (MW)

LOVE AND KISSES
eighty-eights

MALE
buffalo
hard ankle
X-Y-N

MALE HOMOSEXUAL
three legged beaver

MARINE BASE
green machine

MARKED POLICE CAR
blue light
snoopers
taxi
Tijuana taxi

MASTURBATE
choking the chicken
if you can't use it, abuse it (MW)

MECHANIC
mik-e-nik (SW)

MEDIAN
grass

MEET
eyeball it (SE)

MEETING PLACE
  meeting twenty
  M20 (SE)

MEMPHIS, TENNESSEE
  Big M (SE)
  River City (SE, SW)

MESSAGE
  copy

MESSAGE RECEIVED
  four
  four D
  four ten
  got the copy
  10-4
  ten roger

METER READING
  copy
  how am I hitting you?
  pounds
  radio check
  read me
  "S" units
  what am I putting on you?

MICROPHONE
  mike

MIDDLE CBer IN A LINE OF THREE OR MORE
  easy chair (NW)
  rocking chair
  sitting in the saddle (SE)

MILEPOST
marker
milemarker
post

MILITARY POLICE WITH CB
green CBer (W)

MILWAUKEE, WISCONSIN
Beer City (MW)

MISSISSIPPI
Magnolia State (SE)

MONEY
greens
green stamps
lettuce (W)
S and H green stamps
trading stamps

MONITOR (LISTEN)
basketball (SE)
copying the mail
ears on
hang out
on standby
on the by
on the side
reading the mail
10-10
we're down, out, on the side

MONTGOMERY, ALABAMA
Monkey Town (SE)

MOTOR COVER ON LARGE ENGINE
dog house (NW)

MOTORCYCLE
two wheeler

MOUNTAIN
hump

MOVIE
flick

MOVING
on the move
rolling
shaking it (SE)
stepping (SE)
trailer trucking

NASHVILLE, TENNESSEE
Guitar Town (SE, MW)
Music City (SE)
Musical City (SE)
Nastyville (SE)
Opryland

NATIONAL CB JAMBOREE
top twenty

NATIONAL GUARD
weekend warriors

NEUTRAL GEAR
Georgia overdrive

NEW ORLEANS, LOUISIANA
Mardi Gras Town
Superdome City (SE)

NEW YORK CITY
the Dirty Side

NIGHTCLUBBING
boogieing

NO
negatine
negative
negatory
suppository (SE)

NO CONTACT
double seven
negatine contact
negative copy
pair of sevens
10-77

NONSENSE
hang it in your ear (W)

OBSCENE GESTURE
finger wave (SE)

OBSCENE OR PROFANE TALKER
bucket mouth
latrine lips (W)
potty mouth (W)
toilet mouth (W)

OBSCENE TERM (euphemism)
duck plucker

OHIO
    Buckeye State

OLD MAN
    O-M

OLD WOMAN
    O-W

OPPOSITE DIRECTION
    back yard
    how we be looking over your way?
    left shoulder
    over your shoulder

OVERLOAD
    fat load

PADUCAH, KENTUCKY
    River City (MW)

PASSING CAR
    blew my doors off
    dusted my britches (SE, SW)

PASSING LANE
    bullet lane (SE)
    bumper lane
    fifty dollar lane (SE)
    green stamp lane (SE)
    left lane
    mama's lane
    milford lane
    monster lane (MW)
    show-off lane (SE)
    sidedoor (SE)

PEP PILL
   cockleburr (SE)

PERMANENT TRANSCEIVER
   base station

PHOENIX, ARIZONA
   Cactus Patch

PICKUP TRUCK
   pick 'em up truck
   pickum-up

PIGS
   four legged go go dancers (SE)

PLACE OF EMPLOYMENT
   salt mines
   work twenty

PLYMOUTH BARRACUDA
   'cuda
   fish (SE)

POLICE CAR BEYOND RADAR
   catch car
   chase car

POLICE HELICOPTER
   bear in the air
   bear in the sky
   bird in the air (SE)
   chopper in the air
   eye in the sky
   mounty in the sky
   sky bear

POLICE HELICOPTER—CON'T.
    sky mounty
    spy in the sky (SE)

POLICE LOCATION REPORT
    backyard
    bear report
    bear story (SE)
    fix
    left shoulder
    smokey report

POLICE ON THE MOVE
    smokey on rubber

POLICE RADAR
    bear trap
    bears are crawling (SE)
    brush your teeth and comb your hair (NW)
    camera
    electric teeth (SE)
    folding camera
    green stamp collector
    gun runner (SE)
    instamatic
    Kojak with a kodak (SE)
    man with a gun (SE)
    picture taking machine
    polaroid
    portrait painter (SE)
    shot gun
    smile and comb your hair (SE, SW)
    smoke screen (SE)
    smokey with a camera
    wall to wall bears (SW, W)
    x-ray machine

POLICE STATION
bear cage
bear cave (W)
bear's den

POLICE STOPPED
smokey dozing

POLICEMAN OUT OF THE PATROL CAR
smokey on the ground

POLICEWOMAN
girlie bear
lady bear
mama smokey (SE)
smokey beaver (SE, SW, W)

PORNOGRAPHY
comic books
funny books

PRETENDING
stupen (SE)

PROSTITUTE
dress for sale (SW)
free ride (W)
little bit (SE, MW)
pavement princess
snuff-dipper
trick babe (SE)

QSL CARD
wallpaper (NW)

RACE HORSE
four legged beast (W)

REAR CBer IN A LINE
    backdoor
    hind end (SE, SW)
    rake the leaves
    watch your donkey (NW)

REFRIGERATED TRACTOR TRAILER TRUCK
    reefer

REQUESTS FOR IDENTIFICATION
    what's your handle?
    who is in the 4 wheeler?
    who is on the mike?
    who's in that 18 wheeler?
    who we got on that end?
    who we got there?

RESIDENCE LOCATION
    homeport (SE)
    home 10-20
    home twenty

REST AREA
    rest 'em up place (SE)

RESTROOM STOP
    coke stop (SW)
    go to 100 (W)
    pull in for a short, short
    10-100 (SW, W)

RETURN TRIP
    backslide (SE, SW, W)
    backstroke (SE)
    bounce around (SE)
    flip

RETURN TRIP—CON'T.
flip-flop
on a *(name of city)* turn
rebound (SE)

RHODE ISLAND
Mini State (NE)

ROAD CLEAR OF POLICE AND OBSTRUCTIONS
brought it on
clean as a hound's tooth (SE)
clean shot (SE)
clear as a spring day (SE)
everything is slick
good shot
haven't seen a thing in your lane
knock it about
land of wonderful (SE)
light's green
put yourself up here (SE)
straight shot (SE)
way is bueno (SW)
we're clear
we're out of it

ROADWAY FREIGHT SYSTEM
Big R

ROSWELL, NEW MEXICO
Cactus Patch (SW)

SAN CLEMENTE, CALIFORNIA
Tricky Dick's (W)

SAN FRANCISCO, CALIFORNIA
Bay City (W)
Frisco

SCANNING CHANNELS
    quick trip around the horn

SCHOOL BUS
    kiddie car (SE)

SEXUAL ACTIVITY
    clean up
    little bit (SE, SW)

SHOWER ROOM
    rain locker (W)

SHREVEPORT, LOUISIANA
    Sport City (SE)

SIGHTED
    lay an eye on it
    shot an eyeball on it (SE)

SIGNAL TOO LOUD
    bleeding (NW)
    coming in too torrible (SE)

SIGN-OFF
    adios (SW)
    clear
    clear after you
    clear and rolling (SE)
    clear there with you (SE)
    cut loose
    doin' it to it, that way (SE)
    down and gone
    eastbound, struttin' style
    eastbound, trailer truckin' style

SIGN-OFF—CON'T.

eights and other good numbers
eighty-eights
eighty-eights around the house
gone
have a 36-24-36 tonight
he's layin', he's stayin'
I'm through
keep your wheels out of the ditches and the smokeys out of your britches
keep the wheels spinning and the beavers grinning
may all your ups and down be between the sheets
nothing but a green light and a white line
O.K.
out
over
put your pedal to the middle and have yourself a ball cause in that northbound lane we haven't see nothin' at all
seventy-thirds to you
ten-ten 'til we do it again
threes and eights
we be toppin' these hills and poppin' these pills
we up, we down, we clear, we gone
we're backing 'em up now (SE)
we're down, out, on the side (SE)
we quit
westbound and just lookin' around

SLEEP

get horizontal (W)
press some sheets (SW)

SLOW DOWN
    back 'em up (SE)
    back off on it (SE)
    back off the hammer (SE, W)
    back on down
    back out of it
    better cool it
    hammer off (NE)
    hammer up
    let your flaps down (SE)
    pedal a little slower (SE)
    pull your hammer back (SW)
    use the jake (NW)

SMALL TRUCK
    six wheeler

SOON
    short, short (SE)

SPEECH DIFFICULTY
    baryphony

SPEEDING CAR WITHOUT CB
    bear bait
    bear bait passenger
    bear food
    bear meat
    four wheeler with fire in his tail
    pigeon (SE)
    roger roller skate (W)
    run interference

SPEEDING TICKETS
    bagging them (NE)
    bear bite (SE)
    bit on the seat of the britches (SE)
    blue slip (SW)
    Christmas card (NE)
    coupon (SE)
    extra money ticket (W)
    feeding the bears
    greens (SE)
    green stamps
    paperwork (SE)
    piece of paper
    spreading the greens (SE)

SPOUSE
    X-Y
    X-Y-O

STAND BY
    lay it over (SE)
    10-10

ST. LOUIS, MISSOURI
    Gateway City (MW)

STOLEN CB
    rig rip-off

STOP
    turn over

STOP TRANSMITTING
    back 'em on down (or up)
    back it on out
    back off

STOP TRANSMITTING—CON'T.
  back out
  back out of it
  cut loose
  10-3
  10-7
  we go
  we went

STRONG COFFEE
  hundred mile coffee

SWITCH CHANNELS
  make a trip (NW)

TALKING TOO CLOSE TO THE MIKE
  overmodulating

TAMPA, FLORIDA
  Cigar City

TEENAGE CBer
  bubblegummer (W)

TELEPHONE
  double "L"
  land line
  T-X

TEXARKANA, TEXAS and ARKANSAS
  T Town (SE)

TIRE AILMENTS
  bubble trouble
  pumpkin (flat tire)
  slick tennis shoes

TIRED
   checking my eyelids for pin holes (W)

TOLL ROAD
   green stamp road

TRACTOR TRAILER TRUCK
   big car
   box (SE)
   bucket of bolts (MW)
   country cadillac (SE)
   diesel car
   18 legged pogo stick (MW)
   18 wheeler
   flatbed
   growed up truck (SE)
   horse (MW)
   old kitty whomper (MW)
   set of doubles
   tanker
   van

TRAFFIC COURT
   train station

TRAFFIC VIOLATION TICKET
   pink QSL card (W)

TRUCK DRIVER
   buddy (SE)
   cottonpicker
   gear jammer
   good buddy
   guy (NE, MW)
   hard ankle

TRUCK DRIVER—CON'T.
    road jockey
    trucking guy (NE, MW)
    working man (MW)

TRUCK GARAGE
    barn

TRUCK HAULING ANIMALS
    bull rack (NW)

TRUCK HAULING BRICKS
    load of rocks (NW)

TRUCK HAULING CUT TIMBER
    load of sticks (NW)

TRUCK HAULING GAS OR OIL
    petro refinery (SW)
    portable gas station
    portable pipeline
    rolling refinery (SW)

TRUCK HAULING LIQUID
    portable can
    portable pipeline
    thermos bottle

TRUCK HAULING MOBILE HOMES
    shanty shaker

TRUCK STOP
    stage stop (SW)
    truck 'em up stop (SE, SW)
    water hole (SW)

TRUCK TIRES
  PF flyers (SE)
  tennis shoes

TRUCKER'S LOG SHEETS
  swindle sheets

TUNNEL
  hole in the wall

TURN
  hang (MW)

TURN AROUND
  bang a Uey (NE)
  flop it

TURNING OFF
  peeling off (SE)

TURNING OFF THE CB SET
  big switch
  cut the co-ax
  pulling the plug

TUCSON, ARIZONA
  Big T (SW)

UNEVEN TRANSMISSION
  breaking up
  wrinkle (SE)

UNLICENSED CBer
  skip shooter (W)

UNMANNED POLICE CAR
    decoy
    dummy

UNMARKED POLICE CAR
    brown paper bag (NE)
    pink panther
    plain wrapper

UNMARRIED WOMAN
    X-L

VEHICLE VARYING SPEED
    yo yo (SE)

VEHICLE WITHOUT CB FOLLOWING ONE SO
    EQUIPPED
    bear bait passenger
    bob-tailing
    latch-on (SE)
    rider (SE)
    rumble seat

VOICE
    modulation

VOLKSWAGEN
    pregnant roller skate (W)

WARNING TICKET
    pink slip (SW, W)

WASHINGTON, D.C.
    Watergate town

WEAK SIGNAL
    hard to pull out

WEIGHT STATION
    chicken coop
    scale house

WEIGHT STATION WORKER
    flight man (SE, SW, W)
    weight watcher (W)

WHAT KIND OF TRUCK ARE YOU DRIVING?
    what's your eighteen?

WIFE
    first sergeant (W)
    mama (SE)
    other half
    warden
    X-Y-L

WOMAN
    beaver (SE)
    chick (NE)
    cover (NE)
    foxy lady
    lady breaker
    mini skirt (SE)
    muff
    quasar
    seat cover
    skirt (SE)
    super skirt
    sweet thing
    wooly bear (SE)
    wooly wooly (SE)

WRECKER
    draggin' wagon
    Tijuana taxi

YELLOW FREIGHT SYSTEM
    super chickens

YES
    affirmative
    Charlie
    Charlie, Charlie
    Charlie Brown
    definitely
    forty-roger
    four
    four D
    4-10
    positive
    roger
    10-4
    wilco
    yo (SE)

YOUNG LADY
    Y-L

CBers 13 Code

13- 1   ALL UNITS COPY AND THINK YOU'RE AN IDIOT.

13- 2   YES, I COPY, BUT I'M IGNORING YOU.

13- 3   YOU'RE BEAUTIFUL WHEN YOU'RE MAD.

13- 4   SORRY ABOUT THAT, BIG FELLA.

13- 5   SAME TO YOU, SAM.

13- 6   OK, SO I GOOFED, NONE OF US ARE HUMAN.

13- 7   IF YOU CAN'T COPY ME, IT'S YOUR FAULT, BECAUSE I'M RUNNING 3000 WATTS.

13- 8   YOU SOUND SO ILLITERATE, YOUR PARENTS COULDN'T HAVE BEEN MARRIED.

13- 9   ARE YOU RUNNING "ANCIENT MARY"?

13-10   I'D GLADLY HELP YOU OUT, BUT I DON'T KNOW HOW YOU GOT HERE IN THE FIRST PLACE.

13-11   HAVE YOU TRIED BLOWING YOUR NOSE? IT MIGHT CLEAR YOUR EARS.

13-12   IT SOUNDS LIKE YOU STILL HAVE FOOT-IN-MOUTH DISEASE.

13-13   YOUR FRIENDS MUST HAVE PINNED YOUR CO-AX AGAIN.

13-14   I KNOW NOW WHAT AN ANTENNA WITH LESS THAN UNITY GAIN SOUNDS LIKE.

13-15   WHY DID YOU PAY FOR A LICENSE IF YOU ONLY RUN 130 MILLIWATTS?

13-16   THE MOUSE RUNNING YOUR GENERATOR MUST BE TIRED.

13-17   THE ONLY REASON YOU'RE ABLE TO GO HORIZONTAL IS BECAUSE YOUR ANTENNA FELL DOWN.

13-18   IF I COULD COPY YOU, I'D BE TEMPTED TO ANSWER.

13-19   ARE YOU TALKING INTO THE BACK OF YOUR MIKE?

13-20   IS YOUR MIKE CLINKING OR IS YOUR UPPER PLATE LOOSE AGAIN?

13-21   GOOD GRIEF, ARE YOU BEING PAID FOR THE WORD?

13-22   IF YOU HAD SPOKE FOR ANOTHER 30 SECONDS YOU WOULD'VE BEEN ELIGIBLE FOR A BROADCASTING STATION LICENSE.

13-23   YOU MADE MORE SENSE THE LAST TIME YOU WERE SMASHED.

13-24   EITHER MY RECEIVER IS OUT OF ALIGN-
        MENT, OR YOU'RE ON CHANNEL 28.

13-25   THAT'S A NEW ANTENNA? I COULD GET
        A BETTER SIGNAL FROM A DAMN
        STRING.

13-26   WHAT A FANTASTIC SIGNAL, GIVE ME A
        FEW MINUTES SO I CAN BRING THE
        MOBILE UNIT INTO YOUR DRIVEWAY
        SO I CAN COPY YOUR MESSAGE.

(copyright applied for)

**13 CODE FURNISHED COMPLIMENTS OF JAMES ESCUE
"THE BLADE"**

NEW TERMS

If you encounter new terms in your own use of the CB, or if you have any corrections of those within this reference, please fill out the form below and send to the address noted at the bottom of the page.

TERM: AREA OF COUNTRY:

_____   _____
_____   _____
_____   _____
_____   _____
_____   _____
_____   _____

Send to: Lanie Dills
         P.O. Box 1444
         Nashville, Tennessee 37202

Est 944   N ठ

Est 30 mi

JS to muller's